Her

Saving
the
Persecuted

BRIAN AND BRENDA WILLIAMS

Raintree is an imprint of Capstone Global Library Limited, a company incorporated in England and Wales having its registered office at 7 Pilgrim Street, London, EC4V 6LB – Registered company number: 6695582

www.raintree.co.uk
myorders@raintree.co.uk

Edited by Helen Cox Cannons
Designed by Philippa Jenkins
Original illustrations © Capstone Global Library Limited 2015
Ilustrated by HL Studios, Witney, Oxon
Picture research by Jo MIller
Production by Helen McCreath
Originated by Capstone Global Library Limited
Printed and bound in China

ISBN 978 1 406 29881 9 (hardback)
19 18 17 16 15
10 9 8 7 6 5 4 3 2 1

ISBN 978 1 406 29886 4 (paperback)
20 19 18 17 16
10 9 8 7 6 5 4 3 2 1

British Library Cataloguing in Publication Data
A full catalogue record for this book is available from the British Library.

Acknowledgements
We would like to thank the following for permission to reproduce photographs: AP Images: Peter Hillebrecht, File, 27; Chambon Foundation, 21; Corbis: Bettmann, 7, Yevgeny Khaldei, 20; Courtesy of Dragør Lokalarkiv, 32; Getty Images: Fox Photos/Fred Morley, 11, Imagno, 30, Roger Viollet/LAPI, 29, The LIFE Picture Collection/Hans Wild, 33, UIG/Forum, 25; Museum of Jewish History: Courtesy of the Hannah Senesh Family, 39; Newscom: akg-images, 9, 14, 16, 22, 26, 31, 35, 36, dpa/picture-alliance, 4, epa/Stf, 34, Everett Collection, 13, 24, Everett Collection/CSU Archives, cover (right), Photoshot/UPPA, 37, Reuters/Katarina Stoltz, 23, World History Archive, 6; Shutterstock: posztos, 1; SuperStock: Library of Congress, 10; The Granger Collection, NYC - All rights reserved., 17; The Image Works: Press Association, cover (left), 8, SZ Photo/Regina Schmeken, cover (background); United States Holocaust Memorial Museum, courtesy of Norbert Wollheim, 12; Wikimedia, 19, David Shankbone, 40; Yad Vashem The Holocaust Martyrs' and Heroes' Remembrance Authority, 15, 8, 28, 38.

The heroes featured on the front cover are Nicholas Winton (left, holding a child) and Oskar Schindler.

We would like to thank Nick Hunter for his help in the preparation of this book.

Contents

World War II and the Holocaust

Millions died on the battlefield during World War II (1939–45).
However, many more ordinary citizens were enslaved, tortured,
starved and murdered for having the "wrong" beliefs or religion,
or being of the "wrong race". This is known as persecution. Their
main persecutors were Adolf Hitler and the Nazis.

WHO WERE THE NAZIS?

Adolf Hitler became Germany's leader in 1933. Hitler and his
Nazi party wanted to make Germany strong again after its defeat
in World War I (1914–18). World War II began in 1939 when
Germany's attack on Poland forced the Allies to stand up to Hitler.
German forces soon occupied much of Europe. In 1941, Germany
invaded Russia. Later that year, Hitler's ally Japan attacked the
United States, forcing them into the global war, too.

Hitler addressing
Nazi supporters,
flanked by
swastika banners.

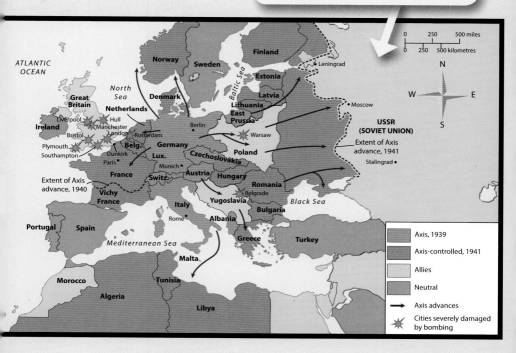

This map shows how much of Europe and the USSR was occupied by the Axis Powers by 1941. The map also shows the cities that were badly damaged by bombing raids.

| 0 | 250 | 500 miles |
| 0 | 250 | 500 kilometres |

ATLANTIC OCEAN

Norway
Sweden
Finland
Baltic Sea
Leningrad
Estonia
Latvia
Lithuania
East Prussia
Moscow

North Sea
Denmark
Great Britain
Netherlands
Ireland
Liverpool
Hull
Manchester
London
Berlin
Warsaw
Bristol
Rotterdam
Plymouth
Belg.
Germany
Poland
USSR (SOVIET UNION)
Southampton
Dunkirk
Lux.
Czechoslovakia
Paris
Munich
Extent of Axis advance, 1941
France
Switz.
Austria
Hungary
Stalingrad
Extent of Axis advance, 1940
Vichy France
Italy
Yugoslavia
Romania
Belgrade
Black Sea
Rome
Albania
Bulgaria
Portugal
Spain
Mediterranean Sea
Greece
Turkey
Malta
Morocco
Tunisia
Algeria
Libya

N / W / E / S

Axis, 1939
Axis-controlled, 1941
Allies
Neutral
→ Axis advances
✳ Cities severely damaged by bombing

HOLOCAUST

The Nazis didn't only attack the armies of the nations that opposed them. They persecuted millions of ordinary people because of their political beliefs, race or religion. Around 6 million Jews were murdered by the Nazis. It was only when Hitler was finally defeated in 1945 that the world learned the full horrors of this terrible crime, which became known as the Holocaust.

WHY DID THE NAZIS PERSECUTE PEOPLE?

Many Germans voted for Hitler, believing in his promises to make Germany great again. But as soon as he came to power, Hitler began persecuting his political opponents and those he believed were inferior to the German race.

RULE BY HATE

Hitler blamed the Jews for the many problems Germany faced at that time, including Germany's defeat in World War I and the economic crisis of the 1930s. The Nazis encouraged mass anti-Semitism (hatred of Jews). They also persecuted disabled people, homosexuals, Roma people (gypsies), Slavs (Poles and Russians), communists and anyone who resisted them.

On 9–10 November 1938, Nazis attacked Jewish shops and businesses. This became known as *Kristallnacht*, the "Night of Broken Glass" (see page 11).

RACE PROPAGANDA

The Nazis used propaganda to stir up race-hatred and to silence anyone who disagreed with their ideas. They censored newspapers, films and radio, and banned "non-German" music and books. The Hitler Youth movement made sure young people also got the message.

In 1939, these German-Jewish refugees escaped by ship across the Atlantic Ocean, only to be refused entry to Cuba at Havana port and returned to Europe.

TURNING PEOPLE AGAINST ONE ANOTHER

The Nazis stirred up fear and mistrust among Germans through this anti-Jewish propaganda. Children stopped playing with their Jewish friends. Parents stopped buying things from Jewish shops. Then, new laws forced Jewish families to move out of their homes. Some families left Germany as refugees, or sent their children away for safety.

DID YOU KNOW ?

Not all German youths were pro-Nazi. The Edelweiss Pirates were young Germans who liked American music, disliked uniforms and refused to join the Hitler Youth movement. The Nazis called them "hooligans". In 1944, 13 youths were hanged for killing a Nazi policeman – 6 of them were, or had been, Pirates.

THE ROAD TO THE HOLOCAUST

Hitler wanted a "pure" Germany, free of what he called "undesirables". At first, the Nazis tried removing Jews from German life and forced them to leave the country. Later, this persecution became more murderous. Some brave people tried to help the Jews, mounting risky rescue efforts before war broke out in 1939.

SAVING JEWISH CHILDREN

Nicholas Winton from London was looking forward to a skiing holiday in 1938, until a friend urged him to visit Nazi-ruled Czechoslovakia to see the thousands of Jews living in refugee camps. Winton and his friends organized eight trains to take 669 Jewish children to safety, finding homes for them in the UK.

Nicholas Winton, in 1938, with one of the children he rescued.

OCCUPATION

Germany occupied Czechoslovakia, Poland and, in 1940, the Netherlands, Denmark and France, among others. Jews and other persecuted minorities in these occupied countries had to live under the brutal rule of the Nazis. As the German army swept into Eastern Europe, millions of Jews were crammed into confined areas in cities, known as ghettos.

From 1941, the Nazis decided on a "Final Solution", which would eliminate all Jews in Europe. Jews were forced to register and then were transported to concentration camps in Poland and elsewhere. Those who were strong enough worked as slaves and many slowly starved to death. Others were taken straight to purpose-built gas chambers and murdered.

Jewish prisoners at Auschwitz, a Nazi concentration camp in Poland. Over 1.1 million victims died there between 1940 and 1945.

Jews under threat

Jews follow the religion of Judaism. They were exiled from their historic home in the Middle East and formed communities all over the world. Everywhere Jews settled, they were a minority and they often suffered anti-Semitism.

When Hitler came to power, many Jews fled from Germany. But Hitler's campaign against the Jews only grew more violent throughout the 1930s.

Adolf Hitler and his Nazi leaders whipped up anti-Jewish feeling to huge crowds of German citizens.

Some Jewish children escaped Nazi Germany aboard ships. These girls reached England in 1938.

FLEEING THEIR HOMES

By 1938, persecution in Germany was so bad that more and more Jewish families tried to leave. Some were helped by foreign visitors who disagreed with the Nazis' horrific treatment of the Jews. For example, sisters Ida and Louise Cook smuggled British visas to German Jews when the Cooks travelled to Germany to watch operas.

Neighbouring countries, including Britain, opened up their borders to thousands of Jews seeking refuge. Major Frank Foley worked at the British Embassy in Berlin, Germany's capital city. He helped more than 10,000 Jews to leave Germany in the months after *Kristallnacht*. Foley was more than just a passport officer; he was also a leading British secret agent, who was recruiting spies and gathering information about Nazi war plans.

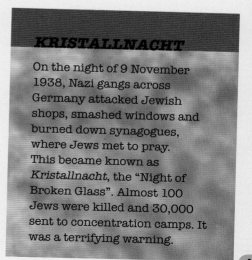

KRISTALLNACHT

On the night of 9 November 1938, Nazi gangs across Germany attacked Jewish shops, smashed windows and burned down synagogues, where Jews met to pray. This became known as *Kristallnacht*, the "Night of Broken Glass". Almost 100 Jews were killed and 30,000 sent to concentration camps. It was a terrifying warning.

ESCAPE TO BRITAIN

The *Kindertransport* (German for "children's transport") was set up to help Jewish children escape from Germany to the safety of Britain by train and ship. British citizens and organizations cared for the children until they could be returned to their parents.

NORBERT WOLLHEIM

Norbert Wollheim (1913–98), a German Jew, arranged travel documents for the children. He worked every hour he could to ensure that as many children as possible escaped the Nazis. Between December 1938 and September 1939, about 7,500 Jewish children left Germany by train to travel to Britain. Most never saw their parents alive again, as they were some of the millions killed in Hitler's concentration camps. The Nazis later sent Norbert and his family to a camp, where his wife and child died. He was rescued by US soldiers in 1945, and settled in the United States after the war.

This is Norbert Wollheim, speaking at a cemetery in Poland where Holocaust victims were buried.

The Nazis burned "anti-German" books, and in propaganda films, posters and cartoons, they portrayed Jews as the hidden enemy, blaming them for causing war.

DIETRICH BONHOEFFER

Dietrich Bonhoeffer was a German Christian who was working in secret with peace campaigners outside Germany. He helped hundreds of Jews escape the Nazis. In 1943, he was accused of plotting to kill Hitler and was arrested. He was hanged in April 1945.

A NEW HOMELAND?

In 1917, Britain supported the idea of a Jewish state in Palestine, which was previously ruled by Turkey. After World War I, the League of Nations gave control of Palestine to Britain. Britain allowed Jews to settle in Palestine, but the Arabs who already lived there protested their arrival. In 1937, Britain decided to limit the numbers of Jews arriving in Palestine. As war clouds darkened, this Jewish escape route was threatened.

Save the children

Children in every war zone faced danger. In the Far East, Japan had invaded China in 1931. British missionary Gladys Aylward led 100 orphans across mountains to escape the Japanese invaders. She showed that brave people could make a difference.

The Japanese invasion of China caused terrible suffering, especially to children.

HO FENG-SHAN

Ho Feng-Shan (1901–97) worked at the Chinese embassy in Vienna from 1938, when Austria became part of Hitler's Reich (empire). To escape, Austrian Jews needed travel documents (visas) from a foreign embassy. Against his boss's wishes, Ho started organizing the visas for families – as many as 900 a month. Ho went on to help possibly thousands of Jews flee Germany until 1940, when he was moved to another job.

Chinese diplomat Ho Feng-Shan helped Jews to escape from Austria. His courage became known to the world only after his death.

CHARLES LUTZ

Charles Lutz (1895–1975) was a Swiss diplomat in Budapest, Hungary. Although the country was an ally of Germany and had passed anti-Jewish laws itself, its Jewish population was initially quite safe. But this began to change in 1943. Lutz saw things were changing for the worse and persuaded the authorities to let 10,000 Jewish children leave for Palestine. In 1944, German Nazis began rounding up Jews, and Lutz gave "safe travel" passes to rescue 8,000 families. He hid Jews in safe houses and jumped into the River Danube to save one Jewish woman from the Nazis. More than 60,000 people owed their lives to his courage.

TRAVEL PERMITS

People working in embassies (diplomats) could issue visas for travel through their own countries. Helpful diplomats handed out as many visas as possible, stretching the rules by putting entire Jewish families on a one-person visa.

Heroes of the Occupation

Jews in occupied countries, like Poland, Denmark and western Russia, were trapped by the invading forces. Jews in Germany's allied countries, such as Hungary, weren't safe either. In Nazi-occupied territory, some Jews joined the resistance. Others were able to escape, thanks to the courage of their neighbours.

German soldiers parade in Denmark in 1940. Occupation meant terror and persecution for the Jews who lived there.

Georg Duckwitz was German, so helping the Jews was doubly dangerous for him.

FOREST FIGHTERS

Living as a Jew in what is now Belarus, Shalom Cholawski had already suffered prejudice before the Germans invaded in 1941. Shalom became a partisan, or resistance fighter, hiding in the forest for years to evade the Germans. He survived the war and later moved to Israel.

GEORG FERDINAND DUCKWITZ

Georg Duckwitz (1904–73) was a German official in occupied Denmark. In 1943, he learned of the horrifying Nazi plans to deport 7,500 Danish Jews to prison camps. He warned Danish leaders and risked his life by crossing into neutral Sweden (see page 21) to set up a "freedom route" across the narrow strip of sea separating the two countries. Many Danes helped, including a cab driver who phoned every Jewish person he could to tell them of the escape route. People even drugged police dogs to prevent them from trailing escaping Jews.

PRISONERS IN THE PHILIPPINES

After Japan occupied the Philippines in 1942, it placed 5,000 US citizens into prison camps like Santo Tomas. Joan Bennett, who was 10 years old at the time, recalled "...people got awfully hungry ... our pet cats and dogs began to disappear...". Many prisoners were grateful to ordinary Filipinos, who smuggled food and gifts into the camps.

DARING TO BE RESCUERS

To be a rescuer or a resister, it took courage, conviction and a cool head. Those who were caught could face imprisonment or dying in a death camp themselves, or they could simply be executed on the spot.

VARIAN FRY

The United States had not yet joined the war when journalist Varian Fry (1907–67) volunteered to go to France in 1940, in order to help the US Emergency Rescue Committee save refugees. Fry's helpers included fellow-American Mary Jane Gold and Raymond Couraud, a tough ex-soldier. They forged travel documents and plotted escape routes for people threatened with deportation to the concentration camps. Fry saved more than 2,000 people from the Nazis.

Varian Fry was eventually expelled (banned) from France in 1941.

Chiune Sugihara and his wife, Yukiko, helped hundreds of Jews escape Nazi Germany.

HELP FROM OTHER COUNTRIES

Abdol Hossein Sardari was Iran's consul in Paris. He helped many Jews escape by giving them travel papers. So did Chiune Sugihara (above), at the Japanese embassy in Lithuania. In 1940, as the Nazi threat to Jews grew, Chiune remembered Solly Ganor, a Jewish boy he'd met in a shop and who'd invited him home to share a family celebration. Chiune and his wife, Yukiko, made travel documents for hundreds of Jews to help them travel east through Russia by train, then to China and Japan, and finally to the United States or Palestine. Solly got a visa but didn't escape. He was sent to a ghetto and then to Dachau concentration camp, but he survived.

A HELPING HAND

Rescuers and resisters were sometimes inspired by religious or political ideals. Others simply cared for those in danger. They helped in many different ways: by hiding refugees in their homes; giving them false names and travel papers; and smuggling them out to a safe country.

ALEXANDRE GLASBERG

Alexandre Glasberg (1902–81) was born a Jew in Ukraine, but became a Christian priest in France. He set up shelters to hide French Jews until, at the end of 1942, he joined the resistance. Glasberg managed to evade capture throughout the war but his brother Vila wasn't so lucky. He was arrested by Gestapo secret police, who believed that they had captured Alexandre. Vila refused to betray his brother and was murdered as a result of his courage. After the war, Alexandre helped Jews move to Palestine.

In 1944, Jews in Nazi-occupied Europe had to wear yellow stars, like these Jews in Hungary.

Pastor Trocmé once said "I do not know what a Jew is. I know only human beings."

PASTOR TROCMÉ'S WAR

Le Chambon-sur-Lignon is a small French village close to the border with Switzerland. Its priest during World War II was Pastor André Trocmé. He and his wife, Magda, believed it was everyone's duty to answer the knock on the door and offer shelter. Hundreds of French Jews came to the village, hoping to escape the Nazis. The Trocmés found the refugees homes and their children school places. They saved more than 3,000 Jews, helping many to cross the mountains into neutral Switzerland.

SEEKING REFUGE

Not all countries in Europe were at war. Some were neutral, and they included the Irish Republic, Spain, Sweden and Switzerland. Refugees and escapees were safe inside a neutral border, so many tried to escape to the nearest neutral, or friendly, country.

Jewish children in the ghetto starved as they awaited shipment to the death camps.

For saving children from the Warsaw Ghetto, Irena Sendler was honoured by Israel as one of the non-Jewish "Righteous Among the Nations".

Many Jews had been forced to live in ghettos since the 1200s, but the ghettos were abolished (banned) in the 19th century. In World War II, however, the Nazis revived the ghetto idea as a way to keep Jews confined in one place. The biggest ghetto was the Warsaw Ghetto, in Poland. Part of the old city of Warsaw was enclosed by barbed wire and high walls – by 1942, the Nazis had crammed 500,000 Jews within its walls. They lived nine to a room and most were sick and starving.

JAN KARSKI

Polish resistance fighter Jan Karski (1914–2000) risked his life to cross Nazi-occupied Europe to see for himself what was happening in the Warsaw Ghetto. He brought news of its horrors to Allied leaders, including Winston Churchill in Great Britain, and US president Franklin D. Roosevelt.

IRENA SENDLER

Irena Sendler (1910–2008) was a Polish social worker who joined Zegota, a secret council set up by the Polish resistance to find safe places for Jews to hide from the Nazis. Sent into the Warsaw Ghetto to check sanitary conditions, she rescued about 2,500 Jewish children, smuggling them out to non-Jewish Polish families' and children's homes. She used the codename Jolanta, but was arrested in 1943 after hiding lists of rescued children and helpers. Irena was sentenced to death but survived because her fellow workers bribed officials to free her. She went on with her rescue work until the war ended in 1945.

Jews are rounded up after the Warsaw Ghetto rising ended in 1943.

THE WARSAW GHETTO UPRISING

In 1942, the Nazis began transporting Jews from the Warsaw Ghetto to the Treblinka death camp, and by the start of 1943, fewer than 60,000 Jews were left in the ghetto. German soldiers marched in to remove 8,000 more victims, but this time they were met by 1,500 Jewish resistance fighters. Led by Mordechai Anielewicz, the Jews fought from cellars, sewers and underground bunkers.

THE LAST STAND

In April 1943, the Germans sent in tanks, heavy guns and flame-throwers to stop the uprising. Anielewicz was killed on 8 May but the last fighters held out until 16 May. In the end, 40,000 Jews were captured or killed. Hundreds were executed, the rest sent to the gas chambers at Treblinka or to concentration camps. Then the Germans demolished the ghetto.

BORUCH SPIEGEL'S BATTLE

Boruch Spiegel (1919–2013) was 23 when he fought in the Warsaw Ghetto Uprising. Spiegel escaped through the city sewers with his future wife, Chaika Belchatowska. His parents, two sisters and a brother all died.

WLADYSLAW BARTOSZEWSKI

Bartoszewski (born 1922, shown right) was a Polish resistance fighter. He tried to save Jews from the gas chambers by working with Zegota (see box on page 23), and telling the outside world about the Nazis' terrible crimes. Bartoszewski had spent six months (September 1940– April 1941) in Auschwitz, so he knew the grim truth. In 1943, he organized weapons for fighters in the Warsaw Ghetto and in 1944, took part in a second Warsaw uprising. He survived the war and became a politician and writer in Poland.

In 1942, the Nazis began to carry out their plan to eliminate every Jew in Europe. They called this "The Final Solution". They started building slave-labour factories and death camps, places whose names are now chilling, such as Auschwitz-Birkenau, Dachau, Treblinka and Bergen-Belsen. Jews, Roma gypsies, Slavs and other "undesirables" from all over Europe were sent to these camps to be murdered.

Hungarian Jews, being rounded up by soldiers at the rail station at Auschwitz-Birkenau death camp, in June 1944.

Oskar Schindler

Oskar Schindler fled to Argentina after the war, but later returned to Germany. He was honoured by Israel for saving so many Jewish lives during the war.

Oskar Schindler (1908–74) was German, though he was born in what is now the Czech Republic. When war broke out, he saw a chance to make money in Poland. He ran two factories in the city of Krakow, using Jewish labourers to make pots and pans for the German army.

By 1943, Schindler had come to despise Nazi cruelty towards the Jews. When he saw Jews being loaded on to trains to be transported to the death camps, he used his business connections and bribed officials to ensure his Jewish workers were not deported.

In 1944, the Nazis were losing the war so they wanted to shut down Schindler's factory, as it was no longer helping the war effort. Schindler had to do something. He made a list of 1,200 Jews he needed to work in a new factory in Czechoslovakia, where his Jews would be safe from the Nazi death camps. This was "Schindler's list". His workers were saved, and in 1945 were freed by the Russians.

Giorgio Perlasca

In wartime Europe, having the wrong identity papers could mean death. However, sometimes it helped to hide your identity, especially if you were Jewish and you wanted to escape to a neutral country. Many escapees were thankful for fake identity papers and "safe passes" provided by rescuers such as Giorgio Perlasca (1910–82).

Perlasca (shown above) was an Italian, working in Budapest, Hungary. After Italy's leader and Hitler's ally Benito Mussolini fell from power in July 1943, the Germans told all Italians to return home from German-occupied countries. This included Hungary, where Perlasca worked. Instead, he stayed and took a job at the Spanish Embassy, where he began issuing "safe passes" to Hungarian Jews. Spain was a neutral country during the war, so it could more easily help to save Jews.

When Perlasca's boss left the Spanish Embassy, Perlasca pretended to be Spanish and took charge. His efforts saved about 3,500 Jews, one of whom told him by letter in April 1945: "You encouraged us when we were close to despair".

TRUE OR FALSE?

Giovanni Palatucci, an Italian police official, was called the "Italian Schindler" for saving 5,000 Jews by giving them fake documents. However, not everyone thinks he was a hero, despite him being honoured at Israel's Holocaust memorial. Some argue that Palatucci was pro-Nazi and hunting Jews, not helping them. Whatever the truth, Palatucci was arrested by the Gestapo and died in Dachau concentration camp in 1945.

THE GESTAPO

Fugitives and rescuers feared the Gestapo, the German Nazi secret police. The Gestapo hunted Jews, tortured captives and sent thousands of "anti-Nazis", including writers, politicians, religious leaders and homosexuals, to concentration camps.

Nazi leader Heinrich Himmler headed the Gestapo and the *Schutzstaffel* (SS) troops that ran the death camps.

Hiding those in danger

Most rescuers were ordinary people, often unprepared for the "knock on the door" that would change their lives. Some gave fugitives food and sheltered them in attics, sheds, cellars or farm buildings. Some helped friends, others hid strangers who became friends.

DOROTHEA NEFF

Dorothea Neff (1903–76) was a famous Austrian actress. In October 1941, her Jewish friend, Lilli Schiff, came in terror to Neff's door. The Nazis had Lilli's name on their list. Dorothea left a fake suicide note from Lilli, to fool the police, and hid Lilli in her flat until the war ended.

Dorothea Neff, in costume in the 1970s. Neff hid her Jewish friend for over three years during the war.

German troops march through the Dutch city of Utrecht, the Netherlands, in 1940. Occupation had just begun there.

WHOM TO TRUST?

Hiding anyone being hunted by the Gestapo was a huge risk. Would their neighbours tell the police? One mistake would mean arrest, torture and probable death. But, even in Germany, some still took the risk.

Elizabeth Abegg was a history teacher. She sheltered Jews in her home and recruited friends and students to help her. She sold her jewellery to raise money and gave Jews false passports with new identities.

TINA STROBOS

Strobos was a Dutch medical student. When the Germans invaded the Netherlands in May 1940, she joined the resistance. Tina hid Jews in her house and found hiding places for Jewish children. She forged passports and carried messages for the resistance.

THE ANONYMOUS COMPANY

The Anonymous Company was a group of Dutch resisters who rescued more than 200 Jewish children. They smuggled the children out of a nursery to save them from being sent to a concentration camp. Because of their efforts, group leaders Joop Woortman and Jaap Musch were arrested. Musch died under Gestapo torture, while Woortman died in Bergen-Belsen death camp.

Ellen Nielsen

Ellen Nielsen (1888–1967) sold fish by the docks in Copenhagen, Denmark. When two Jewish brothers asked for help she hid them, then got them on a boat to Sweden. The Danish resistance sent her more refugees, and at one time she had 30 in her home. In 1944, the Gestapo found out and sent Ellen Nielsen to Ravensbrück camp in Germany. She was ordered to carry children to the gas chambers but refused, somehow escaping execution by bribing guards with soap she had received in a charity parcel. She was eventually freed and went to Sweden.

Hugh O'Flaherty

After the war, Hugh O'Flaherty (circled, with other priests) made friends with the Nazi policeman he outwitted.

Irish priest Hugh O'Flaherty (1898–1963) worked at the Vatican, the headquarters of the Catholic Church in Rome, Italy. He saved hundreds of Jews and anti-Nazis, pitting his wits against local Gestapo boss Herbert Kappler. O'Flaherty hid people in monasteries and convents, the priests' college, apartments and his own home – not only Jews, but also Allied airmen and prisoners-of-war. He was called the "Vatican Scarlet Pimpernel", after a fictional hero who saved victims of the French Revolution (1789–99).

DID YOU KNOW?

After the war, some people argued that the Catholic Church could have done more to save Jews and prevent the Holocaust. Pope Pius XII never condemned the Nazis publicly, saying the Church must be neutral, though privately he did help some Jews.

Raoul Wallenberg

In July 1944, Raoul Wallenberg (born 1912) moved from Sweden to start work at the Swedish Legation (a government office) in Budapest, Hungary. He had been sent on a secret mission: to save Jews. The Nazis had begun to deport Hungary's Jews to Auschwitz-Birkenau death camp. Out of 750,000 Hungarian Jews, only 230,000 remained. More than 100 death trains had already left for the gas chambers.

SAVE AS MANY AS YOU CAN!

Wallenberg set out to save Jews by any means, including bribes. He gave them yellow and blue passes (in Sweden's colours) so they could pretend to be Swedish citizens, and therefore stay safe. He also arranged "safe houses" to shelter Jews on the run from the Nazis.

FREED FROM THE DEATH TRAIN

As the Nazis in Hungary stepped up deportations, Wallenberg got bolder. He stopped trains leaving for Auschwitz in order to hand passes to the Jews crammed into them, then he removed the Jews from the train. Once, Wallenberg prevented a massacre of Jews, telling the German general that if he ordered his men to shoot he would be hanged as a war criminal. It worked.

WALLENBERG DISAPPEARS

By the time the Soviet army entered Budapest in January 1945, Wallenberg had saved at least 100,000 lives. However, the Russians arrested him. Why? Perhaps they thought he was a spy. No one knows, but he was never seen again. The Russians later said the Swede got sick and died, but most people think he was murdered or died in prison. He remains a remarkable hero of the Holocaust.

These are Soviet soldiers in the rubble of Budapest after the city's capture in 1945.

Anne Frank

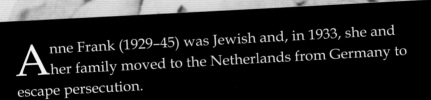

Anne Frank (1929–45) was Jewish and, in 1933, she and her family moved to the Netherlands from Germany to escape persecution.

THE FAMILY IN HIDING

On 10 May 1940, the Nazis invaded the Netherlands and life for Jews became more dangerous. Soon after Anne's 13th birthday in June 1942, her father, Otto, decided the family must "disappear". The four Franks (Otto, mother Edith, and daughters Margot and Anne), with four other Jews (the van Pels family and Fritz Pfeffer) moved into the secret annexe behind Otto's office in Amsterdam. They hid there for over two years. Anne spent hours writing a diary, putting her thoughts and hopes for the future onto paper.

MIEP GIES

Hermine "Miep" Santrouschitz, later Gies (1909–2010), worked for Otto Frank and was good friends with Anne. She, her husband and three others began helping the families in the annexe. In secret, they brought food, clothes and war news to the Jewish "prisoners" upstairs.

BETRAYED?

On 4 August 1944, the police raided the annexe and arrested all eight Jews. Afterwards, Miep ran upstairs to collect Anne's photos and diary. Miep begged the police to free her friends, but to no avail.

Anne Frank died in Bergen-Belsen camp a few months before the end of the war in 1945, and not long after her sister Margot. Of the eight Jews who hid in the annexe, only her father survived.

When Otto returned to the Netherlands, Miep handed him Anne's diary. *The Diary of a Young Girl* by Anne Frank became one of the most famous first-hand documents from World War II, a moving story and a unique insight into life in the annexe.

Anne wrote her diary in these notebooks, which were saved by her friend, Miep.

Fighting back

Alexander Pechersky used his military training to plan a prison uprising.

Many ordinary people were powerless against the Nazis, but some found the courage to fight back.

DEATH CAMP REVOLT

At Sobibor camp in Poland, about 28,000 prisoners were killed each month between April 1942 and October 1943, before Russian soldier Alexander Pechersky and Pole Leon Feldhendler led a prison revolt. With homemade weapons, the prisoners attacked guards, cut barbed wire and dashed for freedom. Some 300 got away, though many were shot or blown up by landmines around the camp perimeter. Alexander Pechersky survived to give evidence in war crimes trials. Feldhendler also escaped, only to be tragically murdered in 1945.

BOMB THE RAILWAYS!

Many experts think that Allied forces could have done more to save lives during the Holocaust. The World Jewish Congress asked the Allies to bomb railways to Nazi death camps and gas chambers, but air force chiefs said it was too difficult.

Hannah Senesh

Hannah Senesh, in uniform with her brother, before her mission.

Hannah Senesh (also spelled Szenes) (1921–44) was a Hungarian Jew who volunteered to be a radio operator and parachutist with the British Army when war broke out. She did this even though she lived in safety in Palestine.

INTO ENEMY TERRITORY

In March 1944, Senesh and other agents parachuted into Yugoslavia and set off to walk into Hungary. Their mission was to rescue Allied pilots and save Jews, but Senesh was captured only hours after crossing the border. She was tortured in prison but refused to beg for her life. She was shot by the Nazis in November 1944.

Tragedy and triumph

In 1945, the Allies liberated the survivors of the death camps and the world learned the full horrors of the Holocaust. The human cost was unimaginable: millions were dead, millions more left homeless and stateless, and families shattered. At least 1.5 million children were killed in the Holocaust.

Even in the darkest times, people somehow managed to show courage and love, and a willingness to risk their lives to save others. The war brought out the worst in some people, but the best in many others.

DID YOU KNOW ?

Adolf Hitler and other leading Nazis killed themselves not long before World War II ended in Europe. Others faced war crimes trials in Nuremberg, Germany, held between 1946 and 1949. Some, such as Adolf Eichmann, escaped to distant countries. Eichmann was eventually captured and executed in Israel in 1962.

Yad Vashem is Israel's Holocaust memorial. Non-Jews who helped Jewish Holocaust victims are honoured as "Righteous Among the Nations".

This map shows how Europe was divided at the end of World War II. In the east, the USSR took control of territory, and put communist governments in countries such as Poland. Germany was split, as was its capital Berlin. In the west, the Allies began the huge task of reconstruction, from which a new Europe emerged.

Timeline

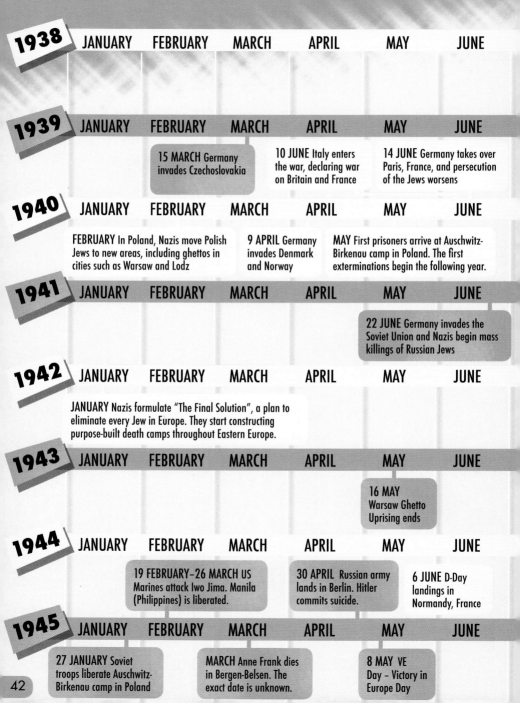

1938 JANUARY FEBRUARY MARCH APRIL MAY JUNE

1939 JANUARY FEBRUARY MARCH APRIL MAY JUNE

15 MARCH Germany invades Czechoslovakia

10 JUNE Italy enters the war, declaring war on Britain and France

14 JUNE Germany takes over Paris, France, and persecution of the Jews worsens

1940 JANUARY FEBRUARY MARCH APRIL MAY JUNE

FEBRUARY In Poland, Nazis move Polish Jews to new areas, including ghettos in cities such as Warsaw and Lodz

9 APRIL Germany invades Denmark and Norway

MAY First prisoners arrive at Auschwitz-Birkenau camp in Poland. The first exterminations begin the following year.

1941 JANUARY FEBRUARY MARCH APRIL MAY JUNE

22 JUNE Germany invades the Soviet Union and Nazis begin mass killings of Russian Jews

1942 JANUARY FEBRUARY MARCH APRIL MAY JUNE

JANUARY Nazis formulate "The Final Solution", a plan to eliminate every Jew in Europe. They start constructing purpose-built death camps throughout Eastern Europe.

1943 JANUARY FEBRUARY MARCH APRIL MAY JUNE

16 MAY Warsaw Ghetto Uprising ends

1944 JANUARY FEBRUARY MARCH APRIL MAY JUNE

19 FEBRUARY–26 MARCH US Marines attack Iwo Jima. Manila (Philippines) is liberated.

30 APRIL Russian army lands in Berlin. Hitler commits suicide.

6 JUNE D-Day landings in Normandy, France

1945 JANUARY FEBRUARY MARCH APRIL MAY JUNE

27 JANUARY Soviet troops liberate Auschwitz-Birkenau camp in Poland

MARCH Anne Frank dies in Bergen-Belsen. The exact date is unknown.

8 MAY VE Day – Victory in Europe Day

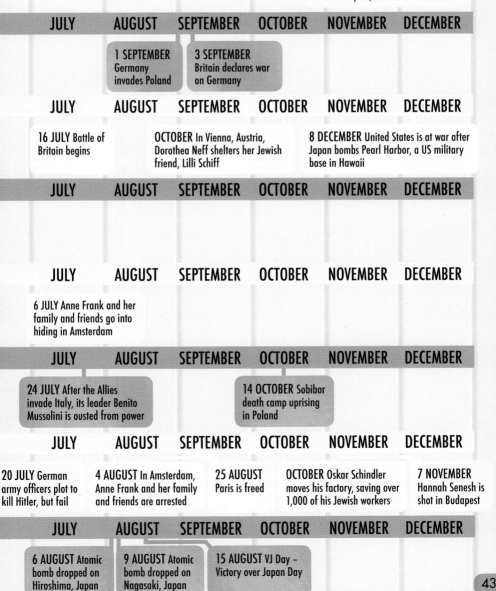

9–10 NOVEMBER On *Kristallnacht*, Nazis smash and burn Jewish businesses and synagogues. Thousands of Jews are sent to concentration camps.

| JULY | AUGUST | SEPTEMBER | OCTOBER | NOVEMBER | DECEMBER |

DECEMBER 1938–SEPTEMBER 1939
The *Kindertransport* evacuation scheme saves nearly 10,000 Jewish children

| JULY | AUGUST | SEPTEMBER | OCTOBER | NOVEMBER | DECEMBER |

1 SEPTEMBER Germany invades Poland

3 SEPTEMBER Britain declares war on Germany

| JULY | AUGUST | SEPTEMBER | OCTOBER | NOVEMBER | DECEMBER |

16 JULY Battle of Britain begins

OCTOBER In Vienna, Austria, Dorothea Neff shelters her Jewish friend, Lilli Schiff

8 DECEMBER United States is at war after Japan bombs Pearl Harbor, a US military base in Hawaii

| JULY | AUGUST | SEPTEMBER | OCTOBER | NOVEMBER | DECEMBER |

| JULY | AUGUST | SEPTEMBER | OCTOBER | NOVEMBER | DECEMBER |

6 JULY Anne Frank and her family and friends go into hiding in Amsterdam

| JULY | AUGUST | SEPTEMBER | OCTOBER | NOVEMBER | DECEMBER |

24 JULY After the Allies invade Italy, its leader Benito Mussolini is ousted from power

14 OCTOBER Sobibor death camp uprising in Poland

| JULY | AUGUST | SEPTEMBER | OCTOBER | NOVEMBER | DECEMBER |

20 JULY German army officers plot to kill Hitler, but fail

4 AUGUST In Amsterdam, Anne Frank and her family and friends are arrested

25 AUGUST Paris is freed

OCTOBER Oskar Schindler moves his factory, saving over 1,000 of his Jewish workers

7 NOVEMBER Hannah Senesh is shot in Budapest

| JULY | AUGUST | SEPTEMBER | OCTOBER | NOVEMBER | DECEMBER |

6 AUGUST Atomic bomb dropped on Hiroshima, Japan

9 AUGUST Atomic bomb dropped on Nagasaki, Japan

15 AUGUST VJ Day – Victory over Japan Day

Glossary

Allies countries, such as Britain, France, the Soviet Union and the United States, that fought against the Axis Powers

annexe usually a smaller building joined to a bigger, main building, providing additional space or accommodation

bribe pay someone to do something they wouldn't normally do in your favour

concentration camp prison camp where large numbers of people, especially political prisoners or persecuted minorities, were imprisoned, often to provide slave labour. Many millions died in the terrible conditions in the camps. There were at least 22 main camps across Germany and Europe, and thousands more smaller ones.

consul government official employed to live in a foreign country to protect and promote his or her country's interests there

death camp also known as extermination camps, these were prison camps set up for one purpose: to exterminate the Jews sent there

deport force a person to leave a country and return to their own country

diplomat official representing a country abroad in another country

gas chamber method for mass murder by poison gas in a sealed room

Gestapo Nazi secret state police, who hunted Jews and "enemies of the state"

ghetto sealed areas of cities in which thousands of Jews were forced to live

Hitler Youth organization set up by Hitler that taught Nazi ideals to young Germans, and prepared boys for the military and girls for motherhood

Holocaust mass murder of Jews and other groups during World War II, including Roma gypsies, Slavs, the physically or mentally disabled and political opponents

invasion when a country attacks another, by sending armies onto its land

Jew person who believes in a form of religion called Judaism

League of Nations international organization founded in 1920, after World War I, in an effort to promote peace in Europe

massacre mass killing

minorities small groups of people, often persecuted for being of a different race or religion

missionary religious person who travels to other countries to spread his or her religion's word

Nazi member of the National Socialist German Workers' party in Germany

neutral taking neither side in a war

occupy take over another country with force. In World War II, Nazi Germany occupied other countries, including Poland.

persecution cruel treatment of someone because of their race, religion, background or political beliefs

propaganda misleading information used to persuade people to believe in a certain political or religious cause

race group of people sharing similar physical characteristics, or history, culture and origins

refugee homeless person fleeing in search of safety, usually from war or natural disaster

resistance groups fighting a secret war against an occupying enemy

safe house secret or hidden house, used by people in hiding

slave-labour (work) camp prison camp where people were forced to work as slaves

undesirable name Hitler and the Nazis used for people they saw as inferior to Germans, such as Jews, Roma gypsies and Slavs

visa travel document, to leave or enter a country

war crime act, such as mass murder or torture, that is regarded as illegal, even during wartime

Find out more

BOOKS

The Holocaust and Life Under Nazi Occupation, Peter Darman (Rosen Publishing Group, 2012)

The Second World War, Henry Brook (Usborne, 2013)

Virginia Hall: World War II Spy, Adrian Bradbury (Collins Educational, 2012)

World War II (Tony Robinson's Weird World of Wonders), Tony Robinson (Macmillan, 2013)

WEBSITE

www.bbc.co.uk/schools/primaryhistory/world_war2
Learn more about World War II on this BBC website.

PLACES TO VISIT

The Imperial War Museum (**www.iwm.org.uk**) has several buildings around the country, including:

Churchill War Rooms
Clive Steps
King Charles Street
London, SW1A 2AQ

IWM London
Lambeth Road
London, SE1 6HZ

IWM North
The Quays
Trafford Wharf Road
Manchester, M17 1TZ

FURTHER RESEARCH

We know about World War II from evidence, such as books, photographs, films, radio broadcasts, posters, diaries and people's memories. Your local public library will have plenty of books about the war, with books by soldiers about their experiences in different war zones. Books and online archives are a valuable source of evidence, from people who were actually there and who recorded what they saw, what war was like and how it affected them. See what more you can find in the way of individual heroism in all these places.

Index